Ask the President

Christy Mihaly

ROurke
Educational Media

A Division of
Carson Dellosa
Education

rourkeeducationalmedia.com

BEFORE AND DURING READING ACTIVITIES

Before Reading: *Building Background Knowledge and Vocabulary*

Building background knowledge can help children process new information and build upon what they already know. Before reading a book, it is important to tap into what children already know about the topic. This will help them develop their vocabulary and increase their reading comprehension.

Questions and Activities to Build Background Knowledge:

1. Look at the front cover of the book and read the title. What do you think this book will be about?
2. What do you already know about this topic?
3. Take a book walk and skim the pages. Look at the table of contents, photographs, captions, and bold words. Did these text features give you any information or predictions about what you will read in this book?

Vocabulary: *Vocabulary Is Key to Reading Comprehension*

Use the following directions to prompt a conversation about each word.

- Read the vocabulary words.
- What comes to mind when you see each word?
- What do you think each word means?

Vocabulary Words:
- aides
- appoint
- cabinet
- impeachment
- military
- officials
- symbol
- treaties

During Reading: *Reading for Meaning and Understanding*

To achieve deep comprehension of a book, children are encouraged to use close reading strategies. During reading, it is important to have children stop and make connections. These connections result in deeper analysis and understanding of a book.

 Close Reading a Text

During reading, have children stop and talk about the following:

- Any confusing parts
- Any unknown words
- Text to text, text to self, text to world connections
- The main idea in each chapter or heading

Encourage children to use context clues to determine the meaning of any unknown words. These strategies will help children learn to analyze the text more thoroughly as they read.

When you are finished reading this book, turn to the next-to-last page for **Text-Dependent Questions** and an **Extension Activity**.

TABLE OF CONTENTS

What the President Does

The president is a **symbol** of the country. What do presidents do? Ask the president!

What is the president's job?

The president leads the executive branch of the United States government. This branch of the government is responsible for enforcing laws. The U.S. Constitution defines the job. It says the president must execute, or carry out, the laws.

George Washington was the first president of the United States.

Some call the president "POTUS." That means "President of the United States." POTUS acts as the Head of State and Commander General of the **military**. It is the president's job to **appoint** many **officials** and talk with leaders from other countries around the world.

Presidents make important speeches. The State of the Union is a big speech to Congress that happens every year. We watch the State of the Union on television. It lets us know how the country is doing.

How does someone become president?

Americans vote for president every four years. Voters in the whole country vote. They vote on the first Tuesday after November 1.

Only citizens born in the U.S. can run. The president must be at least 35 years old. They must live in the U.S. for at least 14 years.

At 42 years old, Theodore Roosevelt was the youngest person to become president.

Who helps the president?

Many people help the president. The vice president and president are elected at the same time. After the president is elected, they pick other people to help lead the government.

Keeping the President Safe
Secret Service agents guard the president's family. Agents travel with the family. Agents even go to school with the president's kids!

One of these officials is the U.S. Attorney General, who runs the Department of Justice. A **cabinet** is chosen to advise the president. Presidents hire **aides**, experts, and report writers. Secret service agents protect the president.

What does a president do at work?

Presidents go to meetings. They study issues. They make decisions.

Presidents announce plans. They sign laws. They answer questions. They work long hours.

Presidents travel. They fly across the country. They meet leaders around the world.

Presidents watch world events. They try to keep good relationships and peace with other countries. Presidents can make **treaties**.

What else do presidents do?

Plenty! Presidents can pardon people. That means forgiving someone for a crime. They can let people out of prison.

Presidents give awards. They visit schools. They visit areas damaged by floods. They lead in many different ways.

Abraham Lincoln
16th President
(1861–1865)

Andrew Johnson
17th President
(1865–1869)

Herbert Clark Hoover
31st President
(1929–1933)

Franklin D. Roosevelt
32nd President
(1933–1945)

Richard M. Nixon
37th President
(1969–1974)

The President Firsts

Which president was first to...

...wear a beard? Abraham Lincoln

...be impeached? Andrew Johnson

...install an office phone? Herbert Hoover

...use a wheelchair? Franklin Roosevelt

...travel to China? Richard Nixon

The Power of the President

How do presidents get things done?

POTUS runs one branch of government. That's a lot of power! The executive branch does what POTUS says.

Presidents can make executive orders. These are rules for the executive branch.

Presidents cannot pass laws. That is Congress's job. But the president works with Congress and makes deals. This might cause Congress to pass certain laws.

Presidents have the power to appoint judges to the U.S. Supreme Court.

What limits the president's power?

The president runs our country, but POTUS does not hold all of the power. Judges look at what the law requires. Courts can tell POTUS what to do.

When the president appoints some officials and makes treaties, Congress must approve. POTUS directs the armed forces, but cannot declare war. Only Congress can.

If the president acts badly or breaks the law, they can be removed from office. This is called **impeachment**. Impeachment involves many steps and trials.

Interesting Things About Being President

Where does the president live?

The president's family lives in the White House. They live upstairs. The president works downstairs in the Oval Office. The White House has 132 rooms. There are meeting rooms, a library, a bowling alley, and even a movie theater!

The Best Part

President Barack Obama liked living close to his office. It's a 45-second walk to the Oval Office from the living quarters of the White House. Obama said that was one of the best parts of the job.

The president works for all the American people—including you! So, tell the president what you think!

Government of the United States

The president is in charge of the executive branch of the federal government. What other positions are in the executive branch?

	Legislative Branch Makes the laws.	Executive Branch Carries out the laws.	Judicial Branch Decides what laws mean.
Federal Governs the whole country.	**Congress** Includes Senators and members of the House of Representatives.	**The President** Works with cabinet members such as the U.S. Attorney General.	**U.S. Courts** Judges work at many courts, including the U.S. Supreme Court.
State Governs each of the 50 states.	**State Legislature** Representatives work at the capitol building in each state's capital city.	**The Governor** Works with many officials such as the Secretary of State and the State Attorney General.	**State Courts** Include the highest court in the state—the state Supreme Court.
Local Governs each village, town, or city.	**City Council** Representatives make rules about how land is used, where roads will be built, and more.	**The City Mayor** Is in charge of the police department, the parks department, and more.	**Local Courts** Judges rule on cases that involve city laws and crimes that are less serious.

Glossary

aides (aydz): people who work with others to help them do their jobs

appoint (uh-POINT): to choose somebody for a job or position

cabinet (KAB-uh-nit): a group of advisers for a head of government

impeachment (im-PEECH-muhnt): the act of bringing charges against a public official for wrongdoing

military (MIL-i-ter-ee): the armed forces of a country such as the army or the navy

officials (uh-FI-shuhls): people chosen to have power and run organizations

symbol (SIM-buhl): someone or something that represents, or stands for, something else

treaties (TREE-teez): written agreements between two or more countries

Index

Text-Dependent Questions

1. What are three powers a president has?

2. How could a president get laws changed?

3. What are two ways Congress might limit what the president can do?

4. Who works for the president?

5. If you were president, what is one thing you would like to change?

Extension Activity

Write a letter to the president. State your opinion about something the president did, about a problem you see, or about an idea you have to improve life for people in the United States. You can send your letter by U.S. Mail or through a White House website. Check for details here: https://www.whitehouse.gov/get-involved/write-or-call/.

ABOUT THE AUTHOR

Christy Mihaly is the author of nonfiction and informational books for young readers, including *Free for You and Me*, a picture book about the First Amendment to the U.S. Constitution. She worked as an attorney for many years. She earned degrees in policy studies and law. She always votes in presidential elections. Find out more or say hello at her website: www.christymihaly.com.

PHOTO CREDITS: Cover: ©Muni Yogeshwaran; page 4: ©Kiyoshi Tanno; page 5: ©Keith Lance; page 6: ©NASA/Bill Ingalls; page 7: ©LOC; page 8: ©U.S. Attorney General; page 9: ©400tmax; page 10: ©usbotschaftberlin; page 11: ©Zerbor; page 12, 13: ©LOC; pages 14-15: ©Mark Hatfield; page 16: ©dcdebs; page 17: ©YinYang; page 18: ©PeteSouza; page 19: ©Annie Leibovitz; page 20: ©Marilyn Nieves

Edited by: Madison Capitano
Cover design by: Rhea Magaro-Wallace
Interior design by: Janine Fisher

Library of Congress PCN Data

Ask the President / Christy Mihaly (Governing the United States)
ISBN 978-1-73162-908-1 (hard cover)
ISBN 978-1-73162-907-4 (soft cover)
ISBN 978-1-73162-909-8 (e-Book)
ISBN 978-1-73163-348-4 (ePub)
Library of Congress Control Number: 2019944972

Rourke Educational Media
Printed in the United States of America,
North Mankato, Minnesota